W9-CKG-222

1941: A WORLD AT WAR

29 USA

"Japanese bomb Pearl Harbor, December 7"

UNITED STATES POSTAL SERVICE

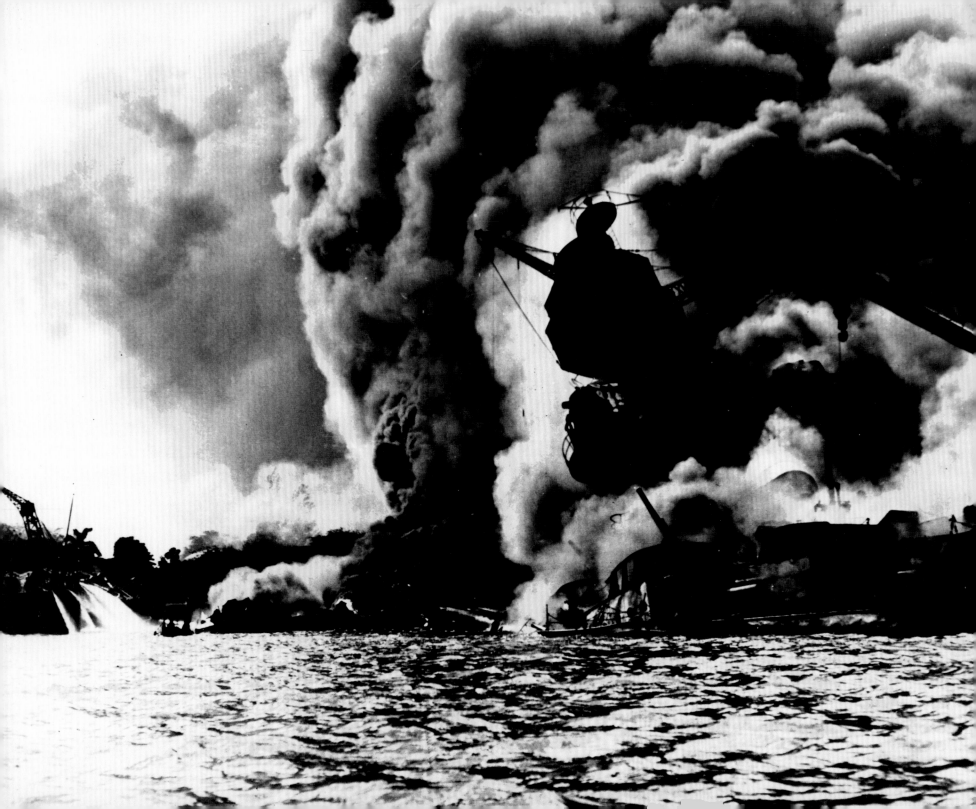

WHO COULD FORESEE EXTENT OF COMING CONFLICT?

It truly was a war that became worldwide. On that Friday morning in September 1939 when Adolf Hitler unleashed his army, his tanks and his dive bombers to destroy Poland, any sensible observer could see that soon the nearby nations of Europe would probably become involved. But who could have foreseen that before the war ended the world would wait breathlessly for news from unheard-of spots like Guadalcanal, Murmansk and Tobruk?

And who in the United States believed that industrial sites like an auto plant in Detroit or a shipyard in Mississippi would be converted into arsenals of democracy to make tanks, airplanes and Liberty ships? And, most important to us as individuals, who realized in those first days that millions of young Americans would go into uniform to serve in places like Anzio, Benghazi and the Coral Sea, or that our aviators would fight life-and-death battles in which the safety of the entire world was involved at places like Midway Island, Saipan and Peenemunde? Or that our amphibious forces would storm ashore at Salerno, Normandy and Iwo Jima?

Chance took me on my Navy duty to 49 different islands in the South Pacific, most of which I had never heard of before, but there I fol-

Best-selling author James Michener, who gathered material for his enduringly popular Tales of the South Pacific *while serving in World War II (far right) added to his reputation as a historical novelist nonpareil with the likes of* Texas, Hawaii, Space *and* Alaska.

lowed with avid interest the great land battles at Stalingrad, the infantry maneuvers at the Remagen bridge and the agonizing warfare at Anzio, for I knew that whereas I fought in the Pacific, at least half of my destiny lay with what was happening in the larger battles in Europe. In the same way, Americans serving in Europe were concerned with the outcome of our land battles on Saipan, our vast naval and air engagements in Leyte Gulf and our bombing runs on Tokyo. We fought on radically different fronts: Normandy, Italy, North Africa, the Mariana Islands and the gates of Japan itself.

As the war progressed I was amazed at the transformations it was producing in ordinary human lives. A shy young woman worked in an assembly line and became so politically involved that later she would run for Congress. I knew young men so distraught by what they saw of war that they resolved: "Come peace, I'm going to study for the min-

istry," or the rabbinate, or the priesthood. Hundreds of thousands, utilizing the G.I. Bill, would go on to college and brilliant careers in law or medicine or politics; in normal times they would never have gained an education. And untold numbers simply found a deeper sense of life and personal direction. I became a writer.

As I look back upon that great war, I am stunned by its duration. Our recent war in the Gulf lasted only 100 hours of actual fighting and was limited to a small geographical focus. World War II, which started in 1939 for European armies, lasted not hours but years, seven of them, 1939-1945 inclusive. For Americans it lasted an appalling 1,365 days filled with such drama, tragedy, triumph and pressure that they altered our national life in almost every aspect. Women gained new freedoms and responsibilities. Moral standards were altered. When peace came, our economy boomed. And above all, what had been an isolationist nation, its people satisfied with their own corner of the world, became one with worldwide interests and experiences.

Now, 50 years later, it is appropriate for the United States Postal Service, on whose Citizens' Stamp Advisory Committee I served for many years, to remember this cataclysmic world event and to pay honor to the men and women who saw it through to victory.

Jim Michener

James A. Michener
Texas Center for Writing, Austin

Troops with field packs hear Hitler orate at Nuremberg, a favorite site of massive Nazi rallies in the 1930s. Such pageantry helped condition Germany for war.

Soldiers (opposite) look through barbed wire at the assault on Poland, which triggered World War II.

WAR AT LAST ENGULFS AMERICA

Edith Wilson chose a black dress and white gloves for her visit to the United States Capitol on December 8, 1941. A deep sense of déjà vu awaited her as she walked into the visitors' gallery of the House of Representatives. On April 2, 1917, she had entered that same gallery as First Lady to hear her husband Woodrow ask the Congress to declare war and thrust the nation into the global conflict then raging, styled "the war to end all wars."

On the day after Pearl Harbor, Mrs. Wilson had come to the Capitol at the invitation of President Franklin D. Roosevelt. He was about to make the same request of Congress that Wilson had made—for a declaration of war to free the world of warmongering tyrants.

The invitation to Mrs. Wilson was more than presidential courtesy. In 1920, Roosevelt had been the running mate of Democratic presidential candidate James M. Cox on an ambitious platform endorsing the League of Nations.

U.S. voters soundly rejected the Cox-Roosevelt ticket in favor of Warren G. Harding, who opposed the League. The ballot was one more defeat for Wilson's dream of a collective security organization to halt aggression. Wilson saw the World War of 1914-18 as a crusade to defang aggressor powers forever, and he tried to orchestrate a forgiving peace that would not provoke future wars. But America's old-world Allies essentially rejected the possibility of a charitable settlement, and Wilson's own countrymen declined to support U.S. membership in his cherished League of Nations.

The League thus began life inauspiciously, without the support of the nation that had nurtured its birth, and it suffered a string of failures as the world's peacekeeper. The Treaty of Versailles exacted territory and imposed indemnities on defeated Germany that kept old wounds open and festering. The seeds of another war were in the ground, but the bitter harvest would not be reaped for a few years.

In the United States the 1920s began like a roller coaster ride. Business was good and getting better, and President Calvin Coolidge in 1925 caught the mood of the nation when he told the American Society of Newspaper Editors: "...the business of America is business." The stock market's steady climb induced mesmeric investment. People who had considered themselves not rich or smart enough to play the market now caught the mania. Clerks and clergy, teachers and matrons borrowed, mortgaged, bought in and learned to chat knowingly about brokers and buying on margin.

Farmers were largely left out of the frenzy, being too busy coping with hard times—and, in some cases, bankruptcy—brought on by the collapse in 1920 of the world grain market.

But prosperity seemed to be on such easy terms with most folks that the country became largely engrossed in making and spending money. The first postwar decade became the "Roaring Twenties," when pursuit of the good life and a good time was "copacetic"—the thing to do. A new slanguage reflected changing values and a flippant irreverence for the past. "Flappers" with bobbed hair, short skirts and rolled-down hose that showed off their "gams" went daringly into "gin mills" to drink "giggle-water" or "hooch" with "drugstore cowboys," then rode off in "struggle buggies" to grapple with morals and each other, sometimes in the "rumble seat" of a sporty coupe.

The press, magazines and motion pictures managed to glamorize the flapper era even when despairing of it. The despairing kept the media on good terms with the vast majority of Americans, who clung to religious faith and the Ten Commandments.

High purpose was reflected in two constitutional amendments that took effect in 1920. One gave women the right to vote, for the first time enfranchising about half of the adult population. The other proclaimed as law what cask-smashing Carry Nation had attempted with her ax—the prohibition of the manufacture, transport, sale or possession of alcoholic beverages.

Prohibition would prove to be a 13-year experiment that didn't take. Too many people were willing to wink at the law in order to buy a drink—or to sell to those with a thirst. Organized crime thrived on this scofflaw attitude and conducted deadly turf wars to protect markets. Disillusionment led to repeal in 1933.

By then the nation had long since gotten off the 1920s roller coaster. The stock market crash of October 1929 had been only the first jolt. The nosedive of stock prices killed confidence in the system, shriveling up consumer spending, cutting consumption, triggering job cutbacks, closing factories and staggering banks with mortgage defaults and savings withdrawals in a domino effect. "The Depression is over," President Herbert Hoover repeatedly assured.

But the whole production process kept failing until 13 million jobless persons roamed the streets, begging for work or simply begging, trying to sell apples to passersby for a nickel or hoboing across the country in railroad boxcars in search of better times and places.

"The only thing we have to fear is fear itself," President Franklin D. Roosevelt said as he took office in March 1933. There followed a whirlwind of emergency measures and initiatives that were known collectively as the "hundred days." Banking reform and public works programs rebuilt confidence and created jobs. There would be insurance for bank deposits and a Civilian Conservation Corps (CCC) to get young men off the streets and out of the boxcars and set them to building roads and improving parks. New agencies and programs gave the public a plethora of initials to sort out and make part of their lives—TVA, PWA, WPA. . . .

It all seemed so well orchestrated, in retrospect, that the grim uncertainties of the moment are overlooked. The President exuded confidence—that was part of his job—but not everyone in the White House could put aside doubts. "One has a feeling of going it blindly," First Lady Eleanor Roosevelt confided, "because we're in a tremendous stream, and none of us know where we're going to land."

Into a socialist or communist state or worse, said critics, and they pointed to a national debt soaring beyond $20 billion! A desperate nation, however, was for trying new recourses, and gradually things changed for the better, first with a rebirth of faith in the system and then with a resurgence of the system itself.

The economy and activities of the country were changed forever by these far-reaching programs. Two measures alone demonstrated a changed America. The Tennessee Valley Authority led the way into federal dam-building and power generation, and the Rural Electrification Administration put the American farmer into the 20th century. Electric lights and milking machines and cream separators went into the barns. Radios in farm parlors and kitchens plugged rural families into the President's "fireside chats," Charlie McCarthy's latest quips via ventriloquist Edgar Bergen and the insights of voice journalists H.V. Kaltenborn and Edward R. Murrow.

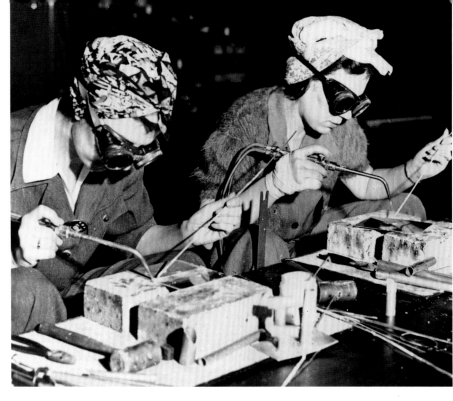

Industry goes to war: U.S.-built arms aided Allies well before Pearl Harbor. Welders at left were among 750,000 women volunteering for jobs after the raid. The nation built miles of plants like this Fort Worth factory that completed a B-24 Liberator bomber every four hours.

A growing capacity for producing electric power, and an expanding use of it in industry and communications, helped prepare the nation for a war it was still trying to avoid. The continuing conflict in China, Italy's invasion of Ethiopia and a civil war in Spain did not long divert American attention from events at home. A ragtag army of some 25,000 veterans of the World War (later to be known as World War I) encamped hopefully in Washington, D.C., in the summer of 1932 in quest of a bonus payment, only to be harried out of town as penniless as when they arrived.

Back-to-back seasons of merciless drought withered Great Plains fields into rootless furrows. When sere winds lofted the loose soil into miles-high roiling clouds, "dust bowl" became a label for regional tragedy. Under skies tinged brown as far as the Ohio Valley, Plains farmers by the hundreds and then by the thousands admitted defeat, abandoning eroded farms to foreclosing banks and the winds, heading west, often to California, where few jobs and a harsh existence awaited. Along the way they picked up a new name, "Okie," from the state that many of them had left behind, together with broken dreams of home.

Labor unions made big gains in the 1930s, though not without violence and death. They devised the "sit-down strike," in which the workers simply occupied the premises of their employer and effectively closed down the operation. The Supreme Court in 1939 ruled sit-down strikes illegal, but by that time labor troubles had eased.

The Supreme Court became a major nemesis for Roosevelt's innovative New Deal measures. Eleven were struck down in hardly more than a year, after 140 years in which the high court had set aside a total of only 60 laws. FDR failed in an effort to retire justices past age 70 and thus tip the court in his favor by new appointments. But then the jurists began to find more merit in New Deal measures and unexpectedly upheld some key laws, including the Wagner Act to protect labor unions, and Social Security.

Increasingly, the movies offered escape to Americans weary of economic woe. A mere two bits or so purchased a ticket to epics of adventure and glamor that almost always served up happy endings. Improvements in sound systems and development of good color film enhanced classics like *Gone With the Wind* and Walt Disney's long-awaited *Snow White and the Seven Dwarfs*, first feature-length animated cartoon in color.

In an era of big-name actors, it is significant that moviegoers made child star Shirley Temple the top box office draw for 1935 through 1938, followed in the next two years by Mickey Rooney, packing them in with his adolescent *Andy Hardy* series. Everybody tried to get seated before the preliminary "Selected Short Subjects," which with any luck would include the latest improbable doings of a mouse named Mickey or a p-p-pig named P-P-Porky.

In major cities, film exhibitors vied to erect the biggest, showiest theaters. But even these palaces could not wall out the real world, because the evening's fare might include a newsreel, showing scenes of floods, strikes and—dependably—the Nazis' latest threat to peace in Europe or the latest victims of Japan's interminable invasion of China.

The newsreel's voice was often that of Lowell Thomas, who introduced America to a cult hero of the first World War with his book *With Lawrence in Arabia* and transitioned from print journalism to pioneer radio journalism by virtue of a momentous and convincing voice.

An evening visit by Lowell Thomas into American homes with his 15-minute radio newscast made him almost like one of the family, a hint of the greater intimacy that would be enjoyed by television news anchors a couple of decades later. He signed on conveniently after the kids had listened to "Little Orphan Annie" and "Jack Armstrong, the All-American Boy." Well before the onset of serious adult listening to such fare as "Gangbusters" or Bing Crosby's "Kraft Music Hall," Thomas delivered his final newsnote and departed with a cheery "So long until tomorrow."

Radio's immediacy was demonstrated when the German dirigible *Hindenburg* burned at Lakehurst, New Jersey, on May 6, 1937, killing 35 of 97 persons aboard. Assigned to broadcast a live account of a supposedly routine mooring, announcer Herb Morrison fought back choking emotion as he described people jumping or falling from the blazing, doomed airship.

The airwaves' power to persuade was proven in a different way on October 30, 1938, by actor-director Orson Welles. Assembling a cast and sound crew around microphones in a studio, he presented a radio version of H.G. Wells' science-fiction classic *The War of the Worlds*, a supposed invasion of Earth by Martians. Thousands of listeners missed the four disclaimers given during the drama, which was scripted as a developing live radio coverage of Martian spaceship landings in New Jersey, near New York City. Panicked listeners nationwide jammed phone lines and gridlocked traffic. A Dayton, Ohio, man telephoned the local newspaper office to ask, "What time will it be the end of the world?"

The lesson in all this was that Americans were relying on their radios for vital information: The age of electronic news distribution was already well underway. The inflection of another human voice could never be adequately conveyed in print but there it was, coming at them from their own radios, as in the weighted words of fatally stricken Lou Gehrig saying good-bye to fans at Yankee Stadium—or the strained abdication broadcast of Edward VIII from Buckingham Palace, bidding good-bye to an empire for the woman he loved.

Advertising at war: As manufacturers turned from civilian goods to arms, ad agencies began to switch familiar brand names to unfamiliar products— Nash-Kelvinator from cars and refrigerators to ocean-spanning flying boats, Firestone from the local auto supply to far-flung fighting fronts swarming with war machines.

Stations and networks were getting the message and starting to assemble staffs and collect and present current events in a more organized way. And as international events of the 1930s pointed increasingly toward another major war, more and more U.S. citizens were getting their news first from their radio speakers, then opening up their newspapers for details and background.

Europe received its first hard clue as to Adolf Hitler's intent in March 1936, when he sent German troops goose-stepping back into the Rhineland in violation of the Treaty of Versailles. In November of the same year, he signed a pact with Japan, ostensibly aimed at the threat of expanding Communism, an echo of a treaty announced a month earlier with Italy. Thus the Berlin-Rome-Tokyo Axis of totalitarian powers was born.

All roads in Germany led to Nuremberg in early September 1937, as trains and convoys of trucks delivered 600,000 storm troopers for the annual opening of the National Socialist Congress. It was the biggest display ever of Nazi power—and the emphasis was plainly military.

Three months later, many Americans braced for possible war with Japan after Japanese bombers and, later, machine-gunning infantry combined to sink the *Panay*, a U.S. Navy gunboat, in the Yangtze River near Nanking. Three United States citizens died. Many older people remembered the battleship *Maine*, whose explosive sinking in Havana harbor in 1898 had set off a war with Spain.

However, Japan claimed the *Panay* had been mistaken for a Chinese vessel. Tokyo apologized and offered indemnity, and Washington accepted.

Austria soon supplanted China as the focus of war jitters. In March 1938, Hitler followed his invading troops into Vienna and declared Austria's "Anschluss"—union—with Germany. A pattern of Nazi expansionism was begun.

Six months later, Nazi ambitions focused on Czechoslovakia's Sudeten region, alleging a need to protect German minorities there. British Prime Minister Neville Chamberlain and French Premier Edouard Daladier went to Munich and agreed to the transfer, in exchange for Hitler's pledge to respect remaining Czech territory. Chamberlain returned to London and brandished the signed agreement as the guarantee of "peace for our time."

Separated from Europe's troubles by the wide Atlantic, Americans cheered the sentiment of a simple song that Kate Smith sang on the eve of Armistice Day, 1938. It was an Irving Berlin tune that he had written for a 1918 musical but then withdrew from the production.

The changing focus of advertising reflected sweeping changes in U.S. life: Names previously connected with safe airliners now tied to deadly fighter planes; a farm truck rugged enough for the Burma Road. All America was going to war, including the animated cartoons and the funny papers.

U.S. postage stamps of the World War II era reflect the nation's concerns about the conflict in such places as China and Poland; America's positive, patriotic spirit, and the country's concentration on defense of its cherished freedoms.

It had never been performed in public before. It was moving, and it was entitled, "God Bless America."

Hitler's guarantee to Czechoslovakia lasted until March 15, 1939, when his armies rolled across the frontier and entered Prague, the capital, in eight hours.

In August, Germany signed a nonaggression pact with the Soviet Union, removing the last obstacle to demands the Nazis were pressing on Poland. The Versailles Treaty had taken away German territory known as the Danzig corridor, giving it to Poland, newly independent. Two weeks later, on September 1, 1939, Germany's armed might rolled across the Polish border. Two days later, France honored alliances with Poland and joined Britain in declaring war on Germany. The lingering embers of 1918 had at last been rekindled. But President Roosevelt proclaimed U.S. neutrality and voiced hope that the nation could somehow still avoid war.

In a matter of weeks the Germans subdued the Poles, despite valiant defense. Poland also lost one-third of its territory to advancing Soviet armies. The U.S.S.R. soon occupied Latvia, given independence from Russia after World War I, and attacked Finland.

The conflict reached across the broad Atlantic in December with a naval battle off South America. Three British cruisers, *Ajax*, *Achilles* and *Exeter*, caught up with the German pocket battleship *Graf Spee* and inflicted major damage in a running fight off Uruguay. With 36 crew dead and 60 wounded, Captain Langsdorff of the *Graf Spee* ordered his crippled vessel scuttled. He later killed himself, and his body was returned to Germany for a hero's burial.

After a quiet winter on the Western Front—the so-called "phony war"—the Allied cause suffered calamitous defeats beginning in the spring of 1940. Germany rolled over Denmark and invaded Norway. In May the Nazi blitzkrieg tactics were put to their biggest test to date—against the Netherlands, Belgium and France. The French Army and a British expeditionary force were soon outflanked. France surrendered and, although the British miraculously extracted most of their army from a trap at Dunkirk—Americans began to visualize how they would live in a world dominated by dictators.

In September, German bombers launched their aerial blitz on London, and suddenly the capital of Great Britain was as much on the front line as an infantryman's trench. Now it seemed to be a poor bet that there would always be an England. And no England meant no British fleet, and the wide Atlantic would not be so wide any more. There was a lot to think about.

A new year did nothing to reassure the country. General Erwin Rommel's Afrika Korps hurled British and ANZAC defenders back toward the frontier of Egypt, raising concern that Germany might seize the Suez Canal. The swastika was raised over Yugoslavia and Greece. Then Germany broke its pact with the Soviet Union, launching an all-out offensive that penetrated swiftly to within artillery range of Leningrad and Moscow.

America's primary interest continued to be across the Atlantic, and when a German submarine sank the U.S. destroyer *Reuben James* in late October, many expected war. After all, it was an unrestricted U-boat attack on U.S. shipping that had sent President Wilson to Congress in 1917 with a request to declare war. But President Franklin Roosevelt was increasingly attentive to developments in the Pacific.

Only two weeks before the *Reuben James* went down, Japan's civilian premier resigned to make way for an all-military cabinet headed by General Hideki Tojo. Events moved fast through late fall, and on November 26, 1941, under strict radio silence, six aircraft carriers of the Imperial Japanese Navy stole out of their base in the Kuriles and set a fateful course eastward. Japanese diplomats in Washington strung out deteriorating negotiations into early December but secret radio traffic to Tokyo, decoded by U.S. intelligence eavesdroppers, pointed increasingly toward war. But where would the first blow come?

The audacious answer transformed Pearl Harbor from a mere place name into an emotional watershed in American history—and at last sent President Roosevelt to the Congress with the request that the country dreaded, yet almost welcomed with a sense of resolving a frustration.

After a paralyzing stroke cut short Woodrow Wilson's 1919 whistle-stop campaign for the League of Nations, his wife sometimes steadied his lagging hand as he signed documents. On December 8, 1941, she heard a request for a declaration of war from another handicapped President, but Roosevelt's impairment was in legs that had been left paralyzed by polio, which he valiantly ignored for a career of public service.

Both Presidents remained strong for a world without wars, a dream that even America's rejection of the League of Nations could not kill in Wilson. In his last public speech, on Armistice Day, 1923, the crippled and dying ex-President told friends assembled outside his home: "I cannot refrain from saying it: I am not one of those who have the least anxiety about the triumph of the principles I have stood for."

As Edith Wilson left the House in 1941, the nation was embarking on another war to validate the Wilsonian ideal of a secure and peaceful Earth. Militarily, the start was not auspicious. The scope of the conflict was infinitely vaster than in 1917, and the time frame had to be thought of in terms of years and years.

Students at Yale University in New Haven, Connecticut, rallied on the evening of December 7 to sing "Over There" and the National Anthem. University President Charles Seymour talked to them of Yale's loyalty and service to America. Then they charged downtown and through the Taft Hotel in an exuberant snake dance that shocked the management for its destruction of window glass and potted palms.

It was a violence of release from the tension of a great uncertainty. But a commitment to war raised greater uncertainties and a prospect of a grimmer, fatal violence that could reach them all. ■

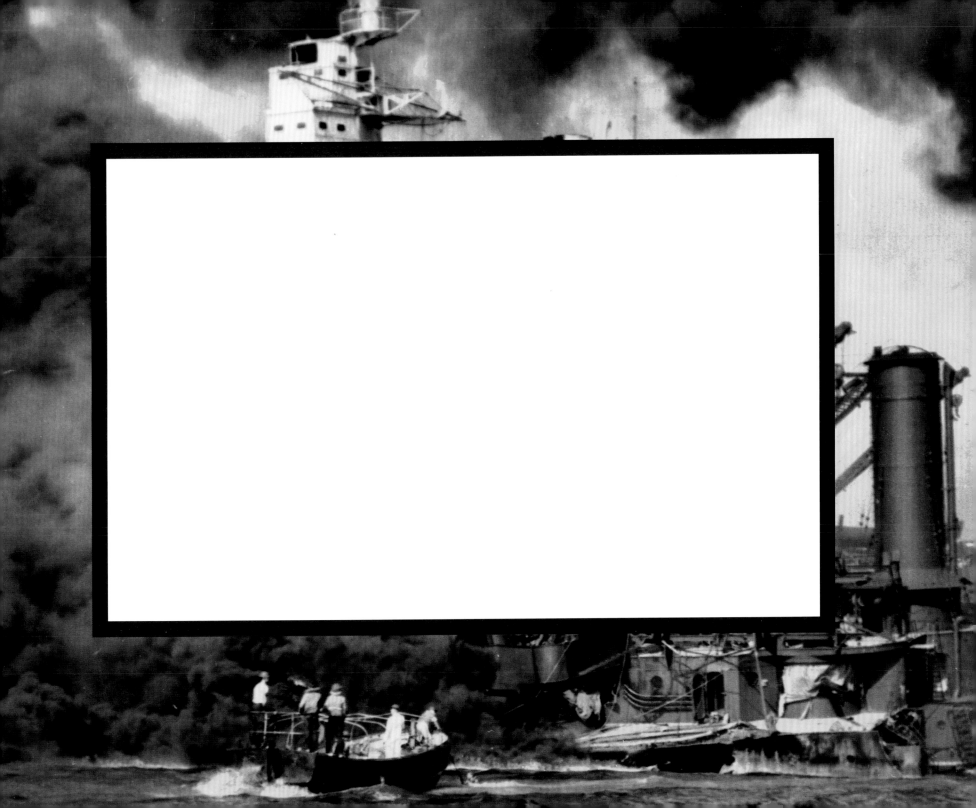

Pancakes bubble
and brown in a
hammered-out mor-
tar shell beside the
Burma Road as Sgt.
Wallace R. Prochot
tries to cook up a
taste of back home
in Gary, Indiana.

Burmese mother
and children wish
luck to the first
truck over the
newly completed
Ledo branch of
the Burma Road.

BURMA ROAD SUPPLIES CHINA

Some of our planet's most formidable terrain said the Burma Road could never be built. Some of its worst weather said it could never be maintained. One of our century's most powerful military forces said it could be bombed out of existence.

But in the summer of 1941 the 2,100-mile overland route from Rangoon on the Bay of Bengal to Chungking, capital of Free China, teemed with trucks. Grinding convoys shuttled arms and food over Asia's lofty spine to a war-beset people despite monsoons, landslides and Japanese air raids.

Such successes in the early years of World War II made the Burma Road a shining symbol in the struggle against totalitarianism. Thus the road carried a freight of hope far beyond mere cargo.

For China, World War II had begun a decade earlier when Japan seized Manchuria and encroached into seaboard provinces. Proclaiming outrage over an alleged Chinese attack, the Japanese in 1936 tried to seize all China. Suffering of the Chinese masses stirred global sympathy as all seaports were captured, closing China's front door on the Pacific.

But the ancient land's vastness plus stubborn resistance stretched the invaders thin and thwarted final conquest. China decided to open its back door, and the Burma Road was born.

Chinese engineers directed some 200,000 villagers in constructing the most challenging section, the 307 miles of cloud-piercing ridges and fever-ridden valleys between Siakwan and the Burma interior. The tasks were awesome—10,000-foot descents into gorges of the Salween and Mekong Rivers; suspension bridges, culverts and small bridges by the hundreds, and unending loops of hairpin turns to complete as part of the original 717-mile section from Kunming, China, to Lashio, Burma.

In the summer of 1941, Chiang Kai-Shek requested American expertise to boost cargo volume over the road, and the U.S. sent dollar-a-year man Daniel Arnstein, the blunt former Teamster who had risen to head New York City's vast terminal system, including 4,500 taxicabs. In six busy weeks, he put a U.S. Army officer in charge of operations, hired U.S. mechanics and dispatchers, put 4,500 new American trucks in service and speeded paving projects. Volume surged toward the desired 30,000 tons a month.

Arnstein had no time for protocol. When asked why he failed to call on the U.S. ambassador to Chungking, he said, "Why should I? I don't know him."

Not since erecting the Great Wall more than 2,000 years earlier had China undertaken so large a project as the Burma Road. Both were built largely by brawn and pickaxes and handbaskets. Both were built to defend China, but the Wall was to keep foreigners out. The road was built to let them and their assistance in, perhaps a hopeful portent in a world still seeking a mutually supportive way to join hands in peace. ∎

Truck and howitzer roll easily across a suspension bridge at the Salween River, once a major hurdle.

Twenty-four switchbacks were required to climb one ridge of the Stilwell Road, which combined the Ledo spur and the Chinese-held portion of the old Burma Road.

The call to arms
abruptly changed
lives and livelihoods.
An Oklahoma City
auto salvage man
simply locked his
shop and posted a
sign. A new Marine
"boot" at Camp
Lejeune, North
Carolina, surrenders
clothing problems
to supply sergeants
indefinitely.

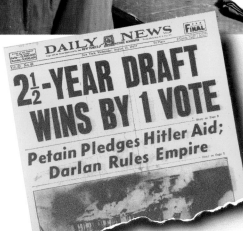

The military hair-
cut is a rite of
passage. No combs
are needed after a
two-minute shear-
ing. "Now I know
how a sheep feels,"
says the recruit.
The barber says,
"Next."

16

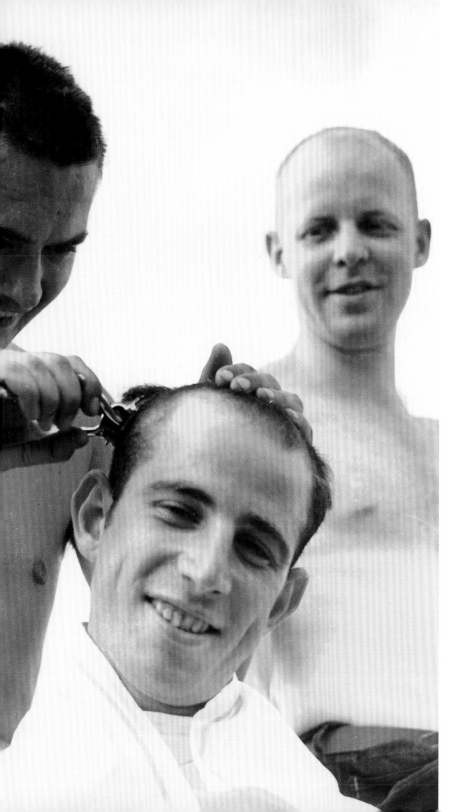

FIRST PEACETIME DRAFT PROCEEDS

By the summer of 1941, inductees in the nation's first peacetime draft were counting the days until their 12-month enrollment expired. Tin Pan Alley tried to sum it up in a song that ran "Goodbye, Dear, I'll Be Back in a Year."

The song's vogue was brief, but the draft lingered on—although only after it had won an extension in Congress by a single vote. By the end of December, the use of the draft had put some 1.4 million Americans in uniform. For the first time in history the United States would enter a major war with some preparation.

But the Selective Service Act had not passed Congress without political trauma. For many Americans, universal military training smacked of Old World militarism. Noah Webster in 1783 said a standing army was "the instrument of tyranny. . . ." From Lexington and Concord on, the citizen-soldier was the American tradition, always ready to trade plowshare for musket at a minute's notice.

As the 1940s began, a crisis known as World War II was towering ever blacker on America's horizon, and debate flared among a citizenry almost evenly divided on U.S. involvement.

A tinderbox issue was whether Congress should vote America's first-ever draft in peacetime.

Men had been conscripted in the Civil War and World War I, but not until after hostilities raged.

But while debate wore on, sentiment tilted toward weary Britain's defiance of Hitler's aerial blitz and against Japan's ravaging of China. On September 16, 1940, President Roosevelt mirrored national consensus by signing the historic peacetime draft into law. By early 1941 the first draftees were donning khaki in real numbers.

In qualifying 16 million men between the ages of 19 and 35, local Selective Service Boards agonized over classifications. Deferments went to key workers and generally to husbands, causing a brief surge in weddings, but most draftees reported dutifully. Lifestyles changed, too, as shorn pates succeeded tousled locks and baggy khakis replaced neat pleats. "This ain't Hart, Schaffner or Marx," quipped a supply sergeant. There was a shortage of shoes that fit and real guns that would shoot. "We are using broomsticks for machine guns and rain pipes for mortars," a general apologized when his Commander-in-Chief, President Franklin D. Roosevelt, came for an inspection. Newsreels showed grinning GIs training with make-believe weapons against a make-believe foe.

But other newsreels of London burning and, later, Russia bleeding and China starving under the affliction of Axis arms, gave purpose to the war games of citizen-draftees and added poignancy to popular songs of the day—Hildegarde crooning "The White Cliffs of Dover" and "Lucky Strike Hit Parade" arrangements of "God Bless America." ∎ **17**

Thirty tons of tank swing aboard a war-bound freighter. FDR likened Lend-Lease to loaning a fire hose to a neighbor whose house was ablaze.

America's ample pantry was also shared. Orange juice concentrate restores a glow to ailing Betty Rothwell, a year old, of Boot Lane in Lancashire, England.

LEND-LEASE ACT PROVIDES ARMS

With her armed forces reeling back on all fronts, Great Britain in early 1941 had a bulldog's bite on survival—despite a bitter reality: The home islands were a battered fortress, arms and stores were depleted, the exchequer drained. As Americans watched, they wrestled a mighty dilemma: how to give vital aid to a valiant people without formally going to war.

Winston Churchill, half-American himself, accurately read that dilemma and sent Franklin Roosevelt a message later described as possibly "the most important letter" he ever wrote. The Prime Minister pleaded with the President to search the Constitution for a way to send help before Britain was "stripped to the bone."

The letter triggered a presidential thought process that crystallized as H.R. 1776, "A Bill to Further Promote the Defense of the United States, and for Other Purposes." History knows it as Lend-Lease, a word so significant that Webster's Collegiate Dictionary enters it with this definition: "The transfer of goods and services to an ally to aid in a common cause, with payment being made by a return of the original items or their use in the common cause or by a similar transfer of other goods and services."

It unleashed an awesome flow of weaponry and supplies.

Not even Lincoln during the Civil War had dared ask Congress for such sweeping authority as this law granted. It included aid to "any country whose defense the President deems vital to the defense of the United States."

Events in Europe had helped the cause. To brief the nation, Mr. Roosevelt had chosen a "fireside chat" during Christmas week of 1940, when London was absorbing one of its worst firebombings. Hitler soon lent a hand by vowing Britain's "destruction" and predicting U.S. aid would arrive too late.

Such boasts were leverage for FDR, who knew how to lead without getting too far ahead. Journalist Clare Boothe Luce, noting that Churchill was known for his V-for-victory sign, Hitler for his stiff-arm salute and Mussolini for his strut, decided Roosevelt's symbol should be a finger held up in the wind.

By canny nudging, he got one of the most far-reaching bills in history through Congress on March 11, 1941. Italian dictator Mussolini reacted with threats of "unpleasant surprises . . . in the Pacific" and Hitler boasted that despite the aid "England will fall." To properly characterize the assistance, Churchill pulled out a Churchillian word, calling Lend-Lease the "third climacteric" of the war, after the fall of France and the Battle of Britain.

History supports Churchill. By late 1942, Britain's lean food larder had been fattened by one million tons and arms supplies rose correspondingly. By war's end, the U.S. had poured $50 billion into the program, which became a keystone for victory and a precedent for massive postwar foreign aid efforts. ∎

Caution with a crane helps inch a weapons carrier into a C-46 for a flight "over the hump" into China.

Late in the war, dried fruit fills a United Nations aid vessel.

Russian label marks cans of yeast tablets going to the U.S.S.R.

19

ROOSEVELT AND CHURCHILL FRAME HISTORIC ATLANTIC CHARTER

For three eventful days a remote bay in Newfoundland held center stage in World War II, but the world didn't know it until later. On U.S. and British warships, President Franklin Roosevelt and Prime Minister Winston Churchill talked over a long list of war-related topics and afterward issued a joint communique on objectives and the kind of world that peace would bring.

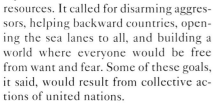

The eight-point statement said people everywhere should be free to choose their own government. It pledged territorial integrity and backed free trade and equal access to Earth's resources. It called for disarming aggressors, helping backward countries, opening the sea lanes to all, and building a world where everyone would be free from want and fear. Some of these goals, it said, would result from collective actions of united nations.

Out of global reaction emerged a name for the document, coined by London's *Daily Herald*, "an 'Atlantic charter'... which discredits Hitler's new order utterly and finally." Endorsements promptly came from 15 key nations.

The historic conference grew from a remark by Harry Hopkins, Roosevelt's ocean-hopping personal emissary, who told Churchill that the President wanted to confer with him "in some lonely bay or another."

They agreed on obscure, foggy Placentia Bay in southeast Newfoundland, and the U.S.S. *Augusta* soon was powering at flank speed with FDR aboard to rendezvous with H.M.S. *Prince of Wales* bringing Britain's prime minister. Churchill soon crossed a short gangplank to *Augusta*, site of all meetings except for a Sunday church service, in which Yanks and Brits joined voices in "Oh God, Our Help in Ages Past."

Back in Washington, Roosevelt found that not all voices were raised in praise of the charter. But the *New York Times*, in an editorial titled "The Rendezvous With Destiny," reflected a growing consensus in the United States. The meeting marked the end of isolation, the *Times* said, and "the beginning of a new era in which the United States assumes the responsibilities which naturally fall to a great World Power."

So where might we view the actual piece of paper embodying the Charter? To this question Roosevelt replied, "There isn't any copy as far as I know. I haven't got one. The British haven't got one.... There was no formal document."

But a message that envisions a just and lasting peace, free of want and fear, lives forever in the minds of men. The Atlantic Charter spoke humanely to the best dream of humanity, and the world can never forget it. ∎

Like old friends even at their first meeting, President Roosevelt and Prime Minister Churchill vowed to destroy Nazi tyranny. Their blueprint for a better world became known as the Atlantic Charter. They held worship services under H.M.S. Prince of Wales' 14-inch guns. Churchill told FDR that "I thank God that such a man as you is the head of your government at a time like this." Behind the seated leaders (far left) stand their two top generals, George C. Marshall and Sir John Dill.

F.D.R.-CHURCHILL WAR DECISION REPORTED

San Francisco Examiner

Endless ranks of wings, engines and shells await mating to fuselage and cannon as production climbs ever higher. American industry's genius for the assembly line—bringing components together at the right time— quadrupled output in the first year after Pearl Harbor. The nation soon had enough arms to equip Allies as well as its own mushrooming forces. In the end, sheer numbers buried the Axis.

DEMOCRACY BUILDS ARSENAL

When President Roosevelt in late 1940 challenged the nation to become "the great arsenal of democracy," he didn't have to explain the urgency to Americans.

Occupied Paris flew a conqueror's flag. The British battled time and fatigue to re-equip and augment forces snatched virtually weaponless from the beaches of Dunkirk. Norwegian troops regrouped in exile in the Shetland Islands, and outgunned Chinese tried vainly to parry Japan's onslaught. Everywhere everybody fighting for freedom's cause was, it seemed, running out of everything.

Despite inadequate planning and lack of precedents for a peacetime build-up, America accepted the President's challenge. Three great assets became apparent: the world's most advanced manufacturing technology, availability of a deep and diverse pool of workers, and a will to get the job done.

The result was the unleashing of stupendous production energies that not only armed and bolstered allies but also ultimately fitted out the most powerful fighting machine the world had ever seen.

Production of new Garand rifles rose from 22,500 a month in 1941 to 52,000 in 1942, fighter planes from 166 a month to 620, medium tanks from 130 to 300 and other aircraft from 490 to 1,600.

By war's end, Americans would build stupefying totals: 296,000 planes, 71,000 naval vessels, 2.4 million trucks.

In 1943, at a meeting in Tehran, Iran, with Roosevelt and Churchill, Soviet Premier Joseph Stalin paid tribute with a toast: "To American production, without which this war would have been lost."

Detroit's production changeover from autos to arms sometimes took only minutes: One worker returned from a washroom visit to find his machine had vanished, having been whisked to a nearby plant where it waited for him to catch up with it.

Good wages and patriotism swelled labor's ranks with older citizens, women and people with unusual abilities. Brewster Aeronautical Corporation of New Jersey, for example, hired diminutive men to complete riveting inside cramped flying-boat wings.

Typical of the effort's impact, a new Du Pont plant in Charlestown, Indiana, pop. 939, brought 15,000 jobs, triggering a boom that outstripped housing, schools, utilities and most public services.

Despite difficulties, democracy's arsenal grew, benefiting from the team play of researchers, managers, economists, military officers, public officials and workers. Meshing talents and resources, they overcame problems and launched output on a skyrocketing trajectory.

Preponderance of production helped keep Allied Forces in the war against tyranny and gave America the weapons to fight in the showdown to come. ∎

The shift changes at a Pennsylvania smelter. Key plants never closed. Workers in sensitive industries wore identification badges.

U.S.S. REUBEN JAMES IS SUNK

First U.S. warship lost in World War II, the Reuben James *became a litmus test for Americans: Many were ready to declare war after this deliberate torpedoing that killed two-thirds of the crew.*

Desperate moments in flaming, oily waters faced survivors of many North Atlantic attacks, like this crew of H.M.S. Glowworm, *before they struggled onto rescue vessels.*

Reuben James *sailor wears smile after rescue.*

SAVE 44 FROM DESTROYER

T he cold and stormy North Atlantic increasingly became the critical arena where the fate of fortress Britain might be decided. Like fortresses of old, that island nation was moated all around, and the besiegers across the Channel were poised to attack.

All help had to come over the broad ocean, chiefly from the United States and Canada, but the Atlantic teemed with the most formidable wolf packs of submarines ever sent to sea. In three months the U-boats sank or captured 22 ships and their vital cargoes. The lifeline from the West might be broken.

But in 1940 the U.S. had traded 50 over-age American destroyers to Britain for 99-year leases on bases. And, by mid-1941 the U.S. Lend-Lease program was able to shuttle substantial aid to Britain. But the delivery end of the supply line lay across 3,000 watery miles that the U-boat fleet was fast converting into a German sea.

The President maneuvered to thwart that ambition by announcing that the United States Navy, already convoying American freighters on their first 1,000 miles into the Atlantic, now would extend its reach to Iceland, where U.S. Marines had landed in July. Since British and Canadian merchantmen tagged onto U.S. convoys, it became only a matter of time until a U-boat skipper's periscope view failed to distinguish between enemy Britons and officially neutral Americans.

In April the destroyer *Niblick* fended off a U-boat with depth charges while saving seamen from a torpedoed Dutch freighter, and in mid-October the U.S.S. *Kearny*, one of the Navy's newest and best destroyers, managed to stay afloat after a torpedo hit amidships.

A stunning blow came less than two weeks later in frigid waters west of Iceland. As the U.S.S. *Reuben James* turned to check out a suspected sub, she took a portside torpedo that blew up one of her ammunition magazines. The forward part disintegrated; the aft sank in five minutes. Of 152 men aboard, only 44 who escaped into the oily, flaming waves lived until picked up.

An old four-stack destroyer of the same vintage traded to Britain for bases, the *Reuben James* was named for a hero of America's war against North Africa's Barbary pirates seven-score years earlier. President Thomas Jefferson had audaciously dispatched the young United States Navy to the western Mediterranean to assert the right of freedom of the seas. Americans of 1941 saw a parallel in the threat to shipping posed by Nazi U-boats and raised an outcry for war.

President Roosevelt, still wary of lingering isolationist clout, sought to shunt the clamor into increased preparations and supplying of Allies.

But as Americans increasingly saw war as a virtual certainty, they found their feelings voiced in a Woody Guthrie song: *What were their names, tell me what were their names? Did you have a friend on the good Reuben James?* ■

U.S. LONG RANGE BOMBER
B-17 E

U.S. FIGHTER
P-38 E

U.S. FIGHTER
P-40 E
(Br. KITTYHAWK)

RECOGNITION FEATURES

RESTRICTED

Could enemy planes darken U.S. skies? Civil Defense said yes—and set up a network of spotters like this Connecticut "sky pilot." He studies aircraft silhouettes to aid identification.

Working long hours with no pay, thousands of volunteers studied Civil Defense booklet to be better prepared.

WHAT CAN I DO

THE CITIZEN'S HANDBOOK FOR WAR

ISSUED BY
UNITED STATES OFFICE OF CIVILIAN DEFENSE

26

CIVIL DEFENSE ACTIVITIES BEGIN

As 1941 began, the world knew that General Billy Mitchell had been right. The maverick Army flier proved to be deadly accurate when he predicted in the 1920s that the airplane would dreadfully alter the next war. Air armadas bristling with guns and bombs would range far beyond earthbound battlefronts to devastate whole cities and countrysides. Now it had happened in Poland and Russia, the Low Countries and northern France, in Norway and China.

If that kind of war came to America, Americans would need more than armies and navies to meet it. They would need people and gear to signal and enforce blackouts, drive ambulances, help police and firemen in emergencies and keep a 24-hour vigil on the skies for unfriendly planes. President Roosevelt recognized that need on May 20, 1941, when he signed an Executive Order creating the Office of Civil Defense.

He named flamboyant New York Mayor Fiorello LaGuardia as the first Director. A World War I aviator, LaGuardia had been a defense witness in General Mitchell's 1925 court martial, testifying that New York City would be helpless against air raids. Now he set about with characteristic energy to give New York and other U.S. cities the means to survive aerial warfare.

The Germans helped provide early incentive for the agency with one of the Luftwaffe's worst bombings of Britain. And the Japanese soon would lob shells at Seattle and Santa Barbara from submarines and send 15 carrier-based Zeros to try to bomb Los Angeles.

With or without enemy goading, Americans were more than ready to sign up in the Civil Defense corps. Eager to find a place in the global struggle, millions volunteered; aircraft spotting alone enlisted the services of 1.5 million persons. When Col. Lemuel Boles scheduled an air raid warden recruitment meeting in Washington, D.C., some 3,000 volunteers tried to crowd into a hall that would hold 200.

Air raid wardens received a tin hat, flashlight and an armband displaying the CD's white triangle on a deep blue circle. Training drills could take on aspects of amateur theatricals as designated wounded submitted to enthusiastic experiments in ministering and bandaging. In a *New Yorker* cartoon of the day, a wife reminds her husband to come home early: "Remember, I promised you for the air raid drill tonight. You're to be a victim pinned under a pole in front of the A&P."

Such rehearsals seemed nearer to grim reality in coastal cities after U-boats sank ships virtually in sight of land. Nighttime skyglow from city lights could silhouette surface vessels, so brownouts darkened streets patrolled by the lonely air raid wardens in Atlantic City and Miami and Savannah.

But happily, the U.S. never knew the necessity of the years of blackouts that Europe endured. ■

World's most imposing skyline darkens during a test blackout in New York City. U-boats, not planes, forced brownouts of East Coast cities to avoid surface vessels being targeted against lighted shorelines. Lights of ferryboats streak the waters in the lower view.

A Minneapolis basement becomes headquarters of an air raid warden and his team.

FIRST LIBERTY SHIP DELIVERED

United States shipbuilders knew from the outset that they were in a race, and at first the enemy was winning: German U-boats were sinking vessels faster than they could be replaced.

But like good distance runners, the American shipyards started strong and never looked back. By December 1941 they were launching a ship a day, and a year later they were sending them out faster than the enemy could sink them. Merchant-ship construction soared from 1 million tons in 1941 to 19 million tons only two years later. In all, the war years saw 5,425 cargo vessels constructed.

About one-half were called Liberty ships, and the prototype was no maritime beauty. She measured 441 feet long, a homely version of a British tramp steamer. Her old-fashioned steam engines could drive her at no more than 12 knots, but she could go 17,000 miles without refueling and deliver 10,000 tons of cargo almost anywhere in the world. In sufficient numbers she could keep vital supply arteries open to overseas Allies and to the nation's farthest battlefronts.

The challenge of how fast a ship could be built produced an unlikely hero. Portly, balding construction contractor Henry J. Kaiser had finished the giant Bonneville and Boulder Dams far ahead of schedule.

Turning to shipbuilding, he set plants across the U.S. to making standardized, key-numbered parts that he stockpiled at his West Coast yards. The stockpiles fed parts by the numbers to new hulls, which seemed to grow magically under the swinging arms of giant cranes, the biggest ever built.

The workers likewise had been assembled from all over the country—pipefitters from Keokuk, riveters from Knoxville, welders from Texarkana. San Diego's population doubled; the San Francisco Bay area teemed with desperate newcomers seeking housing. Some shared beds in relays, arranged around which of three eight-hour shifts they worked in the shipyards that never stopped.

Some bedless folks settled for the upholstered seat of a movie theater that showed "swing-shift matinees" from midnight to 4 a.m. Almost every family in America seemed to have a parent, uncle, or cousin in the shipyards, where the pay was good, morale was high and output was always outdistancing last month's records.

Any vessel delivered in less than 200 days was considered good in 1941. By 1942 the mark was 105 days and shrinking. Finally, with Mr. Kaiser showing the way, yards had to beat 24 days' assembly time to raise approving eyebrows. The best recorded time was 80 hours.

Henry Kaiser was given the punchline in a joke that reflected American shipbuilders' fame for speed. A woman stepped forward with a bottle of champagne to christen a ship, only to discover that the keel had not yet been laid. "What shall I do now?" she asked Mr. Kaiser, who replied, "Just start swinging." ∎

One of the miracles of U.S. production was the Liberty ship, a versatile cargo vessel. Guided by Maritime Commission Chairman Emory S. Land and spurred by the prefabrication genius of Henry J. Kaiser (top), the country produced 2,710 of these "Ugly Ducklings."

Workers of the miracle included shipbuilders at the Bethlehem Fairfield yards. In September 1941 they sent the first Liberty ship down the ways, and it was formally delivered on December 30. It was appropriately named the Patrick Henry. In less than a year, new ships were being launched so fast that finding names was a problem.

Soldiers and sailors risk explosion and fire at Ford Island Naval Air Station to save planes bunched on ramps to prevent sabotage. Almost no U.S. fliers got airborne. As battleships burned in

Pearl Harbor, rumors of imminent invasion panicked many. Tide of messages overwhelmed radio channels and telephone switchboards as news of the attack began to reach an incredulous nation.

PEARL HARBOR IS ATTACKED

Even after half a century, the events of Sunday, December 7, 1941, still carry the shock of a tidal wave. Japanese bombers and torpedo planes had audaciously and methodically attacked America's most powerful warships in Pearl Harbor. After an hour and 50 minutes of fury, eight battleships and three cruisers were sunk or damaged, 188 planes were destroyed, mostly on the ground, and some 2,400 Americans were dead, many in naval vessels turned watery tombs.

It wasn't supposed to happen like that, and it wasn't supposed to happen at Pearl Harbor. More likely targets were U.S. bases in the western Pacific, near Southeast Asia.

"My God! This can't be true," said Navy Secretary Frank Knox, reacting to news of the attack. "This must mean the Philippines." "No sir," Admiral Harold Stark told him, "This is Pearl."

The news made perfect sense to Japanese militarists. Since 1931 a final-exam question for every class at that nation's naval academy had been: "How would you carry out a surprise attack on Pearl Harbor?" An American carrier supplied the answer during 1932 maneuvers by sneaking past a line of destroyers and launching planes for a dawn strike that "sank" the Navy's anchored might. A memo describing that exercise found its way into Japanese naval files.

Americans in the 1930s remained largely oblivious to rising Japanese military power and knew that island nation more by the cheap toys and gewgaws that flooded U.S. markets. "Made in Japan" connoted poor workmanship. Condescension may have been a factor in U.S. failure to take Japanese threats seriously, despite numerous signals picked up in late fall that an attack was shaping.

At 2:20 p.m. on Sunday, December 7, Steve Early, presidential press secretary, set up a conference call to wire services, and the incredible news began to roll out across an incredulous nation. That instant became a watershed in time for the nation, a moment that people would later cite with sharp recall of what they were doing and how they felt when the momentous word overtook them.

John F. Kennedy heard it on a car radio. An urgent phone call cut short a nap for Dwight D. Eisenhower. Winston Churchill phoned Franklin Roosevelt: "Mr. President, what's this about Japan?" FDR responded: "It's quite true. We're all in the same boat now."

Chaplain Howell Forgy, apologizing to gun crews on the U.S.S. New Orleans because he couldn't hold services, advised them to "praise the Lord and pass the ammunition."

While most Americans innocently rallied for prompt retaliation, soldiers and seamen on Oahu who had survived the raid were less assured. As the night of December 7 came on, a sentry at Schofield Barracks shouted a challenge three times, then shot his own mule. The gathering darkness was filled with uncertainty. ∎

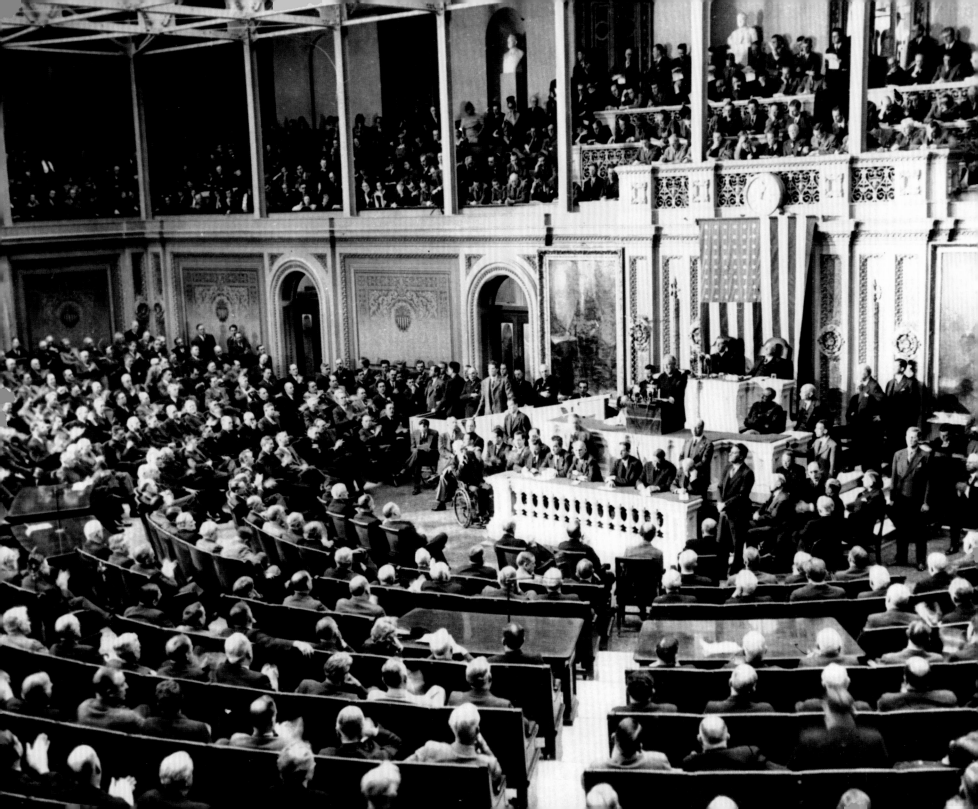

THE U.S. DECLARES WAR ON JAPAN

The America that greeted the dawn on Monday, December 8, had been changed forever. Just one sunrise earlier, the nation had been confident of its defenses but split on whether to jump into the war that was engulfing the world.

Now, grave doubts clouded assessments of American military power. But on the issue of going to war the United States was no longer a house divided. It was time to fight.

President Roosevelt scheduled a Monday afternoon trip to Capitol Hill to put the matter to Congress. He had calmly dictated his thoughts the evening before to secretary Grace Tully, in a White House protected by a doubled guard force.

Eleanor Roosevelt presided over a previously scheduled dinner party, where the President's chair stood grimly empty.

Next door, soldiers labored into the night to put antiaircraft guns atop the old State, War and Navy Building. In his office there, Secretary of State Cordell Hull only hours earlier had received Japanese negotiators Nomura and Kurusu. Already aware of the sneak attack, Hull kept the envoys waiting 15 minutes, then tongue-lashed them for new highs in deceit and showed them the door.

Monday morning found aroused citizens overwhelming military recruiting stations and flocking to blood banks, Civil Defense and Red Cross offices.

Now subversion and terrorism were specters. Anxious security agents wanted a protective automobile to carry the President to Congress, but the U.S. government owned none. FDR had customarily used standard limousines or even an open car, waving cheerily to crowds. Armor and bulletproof glass were needed, and someone remembered that the Internal Revenue Service had seized a vehicle so equipped. It had belonged to gangster Al Capone, jailed for tax evasion. The President rode to the Capitol in the Capone car.

The President's opening words in the tense House Chamber have since become as familiar as those that begin the Declaration of Independence or the Gettysburg Address.

"Yesterday, December 7, 1941—a day which will live in infamy—the United States of America was suddenly and deliberately attacked by naval and air forces of the Empire of Japan. . . ."

In 1917, Congress had debated four days before approving President Wilson's plea for war. In 1941, Congress took only 33 minutes to declare war.

Euphoric over its initial victory, Japan exulted. Adolf Hitler soon declared war on the United States, boasting that the Axis powers could not lose. But Americans found their cue in the penultimate sentence of FDR's war message: "With confidence in our armed forces—with the unbounded determination of our people—we will gain the inevitable triumph—so help us God." ∎

On December 8, President Roosevelt asks for a declaration of war on Japan in a packed House Chamber, under scaffolding for ceiling repairs. Congress acted swiftly and the President signed the declaration only an hour later.

MAPPING OUT THE FIRST YEAR

When the Nazi blitzkrieg swept the low countries into France in 1940, Rand McNally & Company sold out all its large-scale European maps, and there was an attendant shortage of pins with colored heads to stick into them. As Japan's armies swept down the Malay Peninsula in December of 1941, President Roosevelt sent over to National Geographic Society headquarters for a map to locate a town near Singapore that was under attack. The Society complied and for good measure soon sent along a wall case of roll-down maps of all major regions of the Earth.

The war stirred the U.S. Armed Forces to get cracking with mapping. Map historian Lloyd A. Brown described the "miracle of the Army Map Service, how it grew from an almost defunct branch of the War Department to the largest and one of the most efficient map-making agencies in the world." With the Army Air Forces it cooperated to fill in the gaps with aerial photography: "Countless sorties were flown over both enemy and friendly territories for reconnaissance and photographic purposes. In fact, the primary purpose of the early bomber raids of the war was to obtain photography suitable for map-making."

The discovery that much of the world had not been properly mapped came as a shock to the United States and Allies. British and U.S. cartographers divvied up the "unknown" world to avoid duplication and to speed completion of maps accurate enough to stake lives on.

For the American public, much of the confusion arose from the fact that World War II was actually several wars that were in the process of coalescing into one. Since 1931, Japan had been making war on China, and fascist Italy had sent its 20th-century army into feudal Ethiopia in 1935. Each day's events seemed to throw new place names at newspaper readers. Where was Smolensk, or Addis Ababa, or Hankow, or Hanoi? These were places thousands of miles apart, across the planet's major oceans, deep inside unfamiliar continents. Much more than the conflict of 1914-18, this was truly *world war*.

And when the spreading hostilities at last enveloped the United States in December of 1941, most Americans were caught looking the wrong way.

Since German troops invaded Poland in September 1939, Americans showed a preoccupation with the plight of a Europe falling under the Nazi juggernaut. Hitler's strutting minions ruled or threatened the lands ancestral to most Americans. The Soviet Union, deeply stabbed by invasion, seemed doomed. Britain hung on by a fraying thread of overseas supplies. The geography-minded consulted maps to locate the North Africa coastal deserts where seesaw battles raged and the spot north of the Bay of Biscay where the British Navy finally sent the *Bismarck* to the bottom.

Closer to home and more shattering, there was the torpedoing in late October of the U.S.S. *Reuben James*, costing more than 100 American lives. If that didn't provoke the U.S. to fight Germany, then Germany might well be provoked to sink more U.S. warships convoying aid to Britain. By year's end, Lend-Lease had sent 941 tanks and a million tons of food across the Atlantic, plus planes, guns and ammo.

But the decisive confrontation came from the Pacific instead of over the Atlantic. After the country recovered from the initial shock, many people got out their maps and contemplated the dimensions of the Pacific Ocean, the world's largest, stretching one-third of the distance around the globe. They retraced the silent progress of the audacious Japanese fleet toward Pearl Harbor, across a vast, unpatrolled emptiness.

Military strategists and logisticians were staring at those same staggering distances as they faced the necessity of waging war across the Atlantic and Pacific simultaneously. Despite good beginnings in producing more arms and transport, planners had to crank their goals upward by several notches. As Japanese forces swept along toward conquest of all Southeast Asia, the war maps seemed day by day to reflect a bleaker prospect.

For young Americans of draft age, the maps carried a more personal significance. No previous conflict had spread U.S. Armed Forces to such far-flung parts of the globe as World War II promised to do. The Civil War had ranged at times over most of the 19th-century United States, and the Spanish-American had flared from Cuba to the Philippine Islands. World War I had sent doughboys almost entirely to the trenches of northeastern France.

Now young Americans looked at the flash-points of the fighting in late 1941 and wondered. When they finished training and boarded a troopship, would they sail east—or west? "It was a strange feeling," remembered one. "You could wind up getting yourself killed almost any way you looked." ∎

Global war kept GIs moving. Helmet numerals reflect the Army's way of "doing it by the numbers."

1941: A YEAR LEADING DOWN THE PATH TO WAR

January 4 German-born actress Marlene Dietrich, who recently turned down Berlin's request to make movies there, becomes a U.S. citizen.

January 20 Beginning an unprecedented third term, President Roosevelt continues to press Congress for approval of his Lend-Lease bill.

Wartime plot mirrors reality.

February 4 United Service Organization (USO) is founded to serve members of the Armed Forces and defense industries.

February 10 German planes attack Iceland.

February 12 The miracle drug penicillin is given its first successful clinical test at Oxford, England.

February 14 After Italian resistance collapses in the face of a British thrust into Libya, Germany orders General Erwin Rommel to Tripoli to stem Axis reverses.

February 17 Heavyweight boxing champ Joe Louis stops challenger Gus Dorazio with a second-round KO in Philadelphia.

March 11 President Roosevelt signs the Lend-Lease Act, clearing the way for massive aid to Allies.

March 22 Grand Coulee Dam, the world's largest, is dedicated in Washington State.

March 24 Rommel begins an offensive in Libya and in less than a month pushes British forces back to Egypt's border.

April 9 Bing Crosby, Bob Hope and Dorothy Lamour open *Road to Zanzibar* in New York.

April 27 Only 10 days after occupying Belgrade, Yugoslavia, German forces storm into Athens as the Greek army collapses and remnants flee to Crete. The British Imperial Expedition seeks to avoid capture and to escape to Crete and North Africa.

April 30 President Roosevelt buys the first savings bond to aid the defense fund.

May 3 Jockey Eddie Arcaro on Whirlaway wins his second Kentucky Derby.

May 10 German bombs destroy the House of Commons in London while Rudolf Hess, No. 2 Nazi, reaches Scotland and offers a peace plan.

Orson Welles' classic premieres May 1.

May 21 A German U-boat in the Atlantic sinks U.S. merchant ship *Robin Moore*.

May 24 Britain is stunned by the loss in the North Atlantic of H.M.S. *Hood*, with a crew of 1,300, to the guns of the *Bismarck*, pride of Germany's navy. Three days later, British pursuers sink the *Bismarck*, ending one of the great running naval battles of the war.

May 27 Declaring that "an unlimited national emergency exists," President Roosevelt proclaims sweeping powers over labor and industry to speed supplies to Britain. He says U-boats are sinking cargo ships twice as fast as they can be built.

June 2 Rare disease kills Lou Gehrig, New York Yankees' beloved first baseman.

June 16 Harold Ickes, U.S. Defense Oil Coordinator, bans sale of oil to Japan.

"I hope the Red Cross doesn't hear of my sneaking off without my knitting."

June 21 Germans launch all-out invasion of the Soviet Union on a front stretching from the Black Sea to the Arctic Circle.

July 2 Yankees outfielder Joe DiMaggio sets a record by hitting safely in 45 games. He later extends streak to 56 games.

July 7 U.S. Marines land in Iceland, at the invitation of the Icelandic government. Washington cites fears that Germany might take over the island republic.

August 14 After President Roosevelt and Prime Minister Churchill meet aboard warships off Newfoundland, they agree on postwar goals to assure that "all men . . . may live out their lives in freedom from fear and want." The historic statement is dubbed the "Atlantic Charter."

September 4 Nazis announce plans to starve besieged Leningrad into submission.

September 8 British, Canadian and Free Norway commandos destroy coal mines on Nazi-held Spitzbergen.

October 3 Humphrey Bogart plays detective Sam Spade in a new movie called *The Maltese Falcon*. Peter Lorre adds menace in this mystery thriller directed by John Huston.

October 10 Soviet troops halt Nazi drive on Moscow.

October 11 U.S. plans to evacuate 2,000 Japanese from the West Coast.

October 17 General Hideki Tojo and his slate of militarists form a new cabinet in Japan, replacing civilian Premier Fumimaro Konoye, who had been more receptive to negotiating differences with the United States. On the same day in the Atlantic Ocean, the U.S.S. *Kearney* survives a torpedo hit off Iceland but 11 crewmen die.

October 31 U.S.S. *Reuben James* sinks in the North Atlantic after a German submarine attack; 108 American officers and seamen are missing and feared dead, but President Roosevelt does not break ties with Nazi Germany. However, neutrality sentiment weakens, and ties with Britain strengthen.

November 3 U.S. Ambassador to Tokyo Joseph Grew warns Washington of possible sneak attack on American bases.

November 26 Japanese carrier force slips out of bases in the Kurile Islands and heads eastward toward Pearl Harbor.

November 29 Navy beats Army 14-6 in their traditional gridiron clash in Philadelphia.

November 30 British troops sweep across Libya and divide Axis forces, putting Germany's "Desert Fox," Erwin Rommel, momentarily on the defensive.

Rita Hayworth, cotton stockings back rationing.

December 1 Premier Tojo turns down U.S. offers to settle dispute.

December 7 Breaking the quiet of a sleepy Sunday morning, Japanese carrier-based planes shatter the U.S. fleet tied up in Pearl Harbor. Some 2,000 servicemen and 400 civilians die. The nation is stunned.

December 8 A joint session of Congress and a packed gallery hear President Roosevelt call for a declaration of war against the Empire of Japan. Congress complies within the hour and three days later declares war on Japan's Axis partners, Germany and Italy.

December 10 Japanese troops invade the Philippines, landing on the main island of Luzon.

December 23 Wake Island surrenders to Japanese landing force.

December 25 British governor of the Crown Colony of Hong Kong surrenders to Japanese.

THERE'LL BE BLUE BIRDS OVER
THE WHITE CLIFFS OF DOVER

Britain-inspired song scores hit with Americans.

37

ONE ON THE CHIN, BUT NOT OUT FOR THE COUNT

The summer of 1941 was a great season for baseball and its fans, especially those loyal to the New York Yankees and the Boston Red Sox. Yankee Stadium reverberated to cheers for slugger Joe DiMaggio and his record 56-consecutive-game hitting streak. Fenway Park faithful deafened ears in their joy for a skinny kid named Ted Williams and his fat batting average for the year—a whopping .406. Boxing fans roared enthusiasm for Joe Louis, who from January to September defeated seven contenders—six by knockouts—and continued his reign as heavyweight champion of the world.

In retrospect, a mellow aura of a departed age hangs over those happy American sports fans and their heroes, because we of the postwar era live with the knowledge of the grim events that by the next summer would be sending them off to war by millions, almost half a million not to return.

In the summer of '41, many Americans still hoped to avoid the widening conflict. They clung to peace as the norm, despite a tumultuous history that had included more than a 100 calls to active military service, plus 60 foreign expeditions and 76 Indian wars. Historian Henry Steele Commager in 1951 figured the country had "been engaged in major wars for twenty-five years—one year out of every seven of national existence."

But in the summer of '41, barely a generation beyond the carnage of 1917-18, there was a widespread perception

Shooting gallery for Nazi submarines, the North Atlantic by early 1942 offered many a wallowing convoy as periscope targets for U-boat skippers, giving the Allies little to cheer about in the new year.

that the Old World was repeating the tragic mistakes of bloodletting. The United States' most tangible legacy of World War I involvement lay in the beds of veterans' hospitals and soldiers' homes or beneath long ranks of headstones from the Ardennes to Arlington Cemetery. A strong bloc of citizenry looked back across the disillusionment of the victors' pie Treaty of Versailles to George Washington's sage counsel against entangling foreign alliances.

But an equally strong element saw America inevitably drawn into

the sharpening global showdown between democracy and dictatorship, and the country's unpreparedness set off agonies of debate. Will Rogers, with his knack for fetching a wry chuckle from dire headlines, observed: "We are the only nation in the world that waits until we get into a war before we start getting ready for it. Pacifists say, 'If you are ready for war, you will have one.' I bet there has not been a man (who has) insulted Jack Dempsey since he became champion."

More and more citizens were finding validity in Will's parable of champions, impelled by a year in which the Berlin-Rome-Tokyo forces had hurled back democratic defenders on virtually every front. Drawing upon programs launched during 1940 in some instances, the United States began to turn 1941 into the

year of getting ready. Appropriately, seven of the 10 stamps in this commemorative album recall significant steps taken to arm the nation or its allies.

The Atlantic Charter, that evocative statement of aims that never was ceremonially set down on parchment, defined the shared ideals of the struggle. It echoed the freedoms of choice and of access to Earth's resources that had anointed Woodrow Wilson's Fourteen Points of 1918 with high purpose. For those who subscribed to the charter, World War II took on the light of a morality play.

It was a light that beckoned to most Americans, brought up to believe that might does not make right, that the end does not justify the means. It was all summed up in an admonitory verse that hung above the backboards in many

a high school gymnasium across the country: "When the Great Scorer comes/ To write against your name,/ He writes not that you won or lost/ But how you played the game."

For a people holding such convictions, it became increasingly easy to see they were not on the side of Adolf Hitler, who lectured his generals: "In starting and waging a war, it is not right that matters, but victory." And the creed of the Great Scorer did not reconcile with a Japan that would launch a deadly sneak attack before declaring war. There was a code that said you do not land one on your adversary's chin while he stands there flat-footed, awaiting the opening bell.

Thus it was Japan, through a misreading of American character, that finally resolved the United States' dilemma and made it a country of one mind

in favor of war. President Roosevelt perceptively characterized the surprise action as a "day of infamy," a brand that burned purpose into the national will.

An enthusiastic stamp collector even amid the conflict, FDR often took albums with him as he traveled, for moments of updating or perusal. On his final day at Warm Springs, Georgia, before the onset of his fatal stroke in April 1945, he had found time for brief pleasure with his beloved stamps.

The stamps in this album, plus others scheduled during the next four 50th-anniversary years of World War II, are inextricably linked to the history that Franklin Roosevelt lived and helped shape. With his zest for following grand events, he would find special satisfaction in these philatelic salutes to the world-changing events of his final years. ∎

World War II changed the course of stamp artist William H. Bond's life, and but for the luck of timing might have cut it short. A parachute-borne, delayed-action bomb, called a "land mine," destroyed his family's house in east London during the German aerial blitz, but fortunately, the Bond family was safe in their backyard Anderson shelter.

A youthful defense worker when the war started in 1939, Bill enrolled in the Sea Cadets, then volunteered for active service in the Royal Navy at 17. He was attached to Combined Allied Operations in the Mediterranean and as a signalman took part in the landings on Sicily.

The end of the war gave Bill a chance to reassess his life and study art, a lifelong interest. Studying at Twickenham Art College, he found employment in postwar London, working with some of England's leading illustrators in a studio overlooking St. Paul's Cathedral.

In 1954 Bill moved to Canada, where he spent 15 years working in Toronto. He opened his own studio and was soon building a clientele for his color illustrations, portraits and magazine covers.

Bill's work attracted *National Geographic,* which made him a staff artist in 1966. There followed a parade of assignments ranging the world and vastly varied subject matter.

His assignment to design this series of World War II anniversary stamps evoked a parade of long-forgotten scenes across wartime Mediterranean—Algiers, Tunis, Salerno, the many islands of the Adriatic, Trieste. Sent to besieged Malta for some R & R in 1943, Bill found the limited diet less that recreational. "They fed us onions three times a day," he recalls.

Bill, a resident of Arlington, Virginia, is a U.S. citizen, is married and has three daughters.

Rowe Findley's writing of text and captions for this series of commemorative albums brings him full circle with stamps and World War II. Recently retired after a distinguished 31-year career as one of *National Geographic*'s top writers, he was a 17-year-old high school senior in early 1943 when he worked a few months for his hometown post office in Willow Springs, Missouri, dispatching mail to many an APO. Then he turned 18 and ultimately became an APO addressee himself, flying as a B-29 bombardier from Tinian in the air offensive against Japan. He recently revisited Tinian to help dedicate a plaque to the 157 airmen in his group who died in the aerial combat. ∎

Special thanks are extended to the following individuals for their contributions to the production of this book:

Eric Call
Print production procurement and supervision

Wendy Cortesi
Copy editing and research

Col. Charles A. Endress,
U.S. Army Reserve
Historical research

Rowe Findley
Narrative material

Bill Halstead
Editing and project management

Jonathan Kronstadt
Editorial research

Sharon Mann
Composition

Tom Mann
Design, photo editing and production

James Michener
Introduction

Fred Otnes
Cover artwork

Howard Paine
Creative direction

Susan Robb
Picture research

CREDITS: **Front endpaper**—Map of London, Library of Congress. **2-3**—U.S.S. *Arizona* burning, National Archives; James A. Michener photographs, courtesy the author. **4-5**—Nazi rally at Nuremberg, FPG International; German soldiers in trench, UPI/Bettmann. **6-7**—St. Paul's Cathedral in the Blitz, 1941, Popperfoto; London Blitz painting by William H. Bond, ©National Geographic Society. **8-9**—Women welders, Library of Congress; B-24 production, General Dynamics Corporation. **10-11**—Kelvinator ad, *National Geographic* magazine, Dec. 1942; War Bonds postcard, collection of Arnold C. Holeywell; Prestone ad, *National Geographic*, Nov. 1941; Lockheed ad, *National Geographic*, Feb. 1941; International Trucks ad, *Life* magazine, July 7, 1941; Revere ad, *Fortune* magazine, April 1941. **12-13**—U.S. postage stamps, photo by Lauri Bridgeforth; U.S.S. *West Virginia* rescue, National Archives. **14-15**—GI hot cakes, National Archives; Convoy drivers and Burmese family, National Archives; Truck and howitzer crossing suspension bridge, National Archives; "24 Curves", Library of Congress. **16-17**—"Gone to Army" sign, Library of Congress; Clothing issue, Library of Congress; Newspaper headline, Library of Congress; GI haircut, Library of Congress. **18-19**—American M-4 tank, National Archives; British child, National Archives; Newspaper headline, Library of Congress; Loading weapons-carrier, National Archives; Lend-Lease shipment, National Archives; Lend-Lease for Russia, National Archives. **20-21**— FDR and Churchill on deck of H.M.S. *Prince of Wales,* National Archives; Church service aboard H.M.S. *Prince of Wales,* National Archives; Churchill greets FDR, National Archives; Newspaper headline,

Library of Congress. **22-23**—Aircobra wings, Library of Congress; 14-inch armor-piercing shells, Library of Congress; Aircraft production, Library of Congress; Change of shifts, Library of Congress; Identification badge, courtesy Janet Margeson Paine; Newspaper headline, Library of Congress. **24-25**—U.S.S. *Reuben James,* National Archives; Surviving sailor, Official U.S. Navy Photograph; Newspaper headline, Library of Congress; British destroyer *Glowworm* crew rescue, Dever from Black Star; "The Sinking of the *Reuben James,*" words and music by Woody Guthrie, ©1942 MCA Music Publishing. **26-27**—Aircraft identification charts, Library of Congress; Civil Defense booklet, courtesy of "a Gatherin' Historical Papers"; Identifying planes, Eric Schaal, *Life,* ©Time Warner Inc.; New York skyline, Library of Congress; Civil Defense workers, National Archives; Cartoon caption in text, courtesy of *New Yorker* magazine. **28-29**—Henry J. Kaiser, AP/Wide World; Lunch break at shipyard, Library of Congress; Shipyard workers, Library of Congress; Liberty ship, National Archives. **30-31**—Pearl Harbor attack, Ford Island, National Archives; Civil Defense worker at Pearl Harbor, 7 Dec 41, National Archives; U.S.S. *Shaw* exploding, National Archives. **32-33**—FDR delivers war message to Congress, National Archives; FDR signs declaration of war, Library of Congress; Newspaper headline, Library of Congress. **34-35**—The movement starts, Library of Congress. **36-37**—Hemingway book, photo by Lauri Bridgeforth; *New Yorker* cartoon, *New Yorker,* Feb. 15, 1941; *Citizen Kane* poster, Carson Collection; Joe DiMaggio, *The Sporting News; Maltese Falcon* photo, Turner Entertainment Company; Rita Hayworth, Library of Congress; "The White Cliffs of Dover," Walter Kent Music Company. **38-39**—U-Boat commander, University of South Carolina Newsfilm Library; Atlantic convoy, National Archives. **40**—Bill Bond, photo by Gerald Merna, U.S. Postal Service; Rowe Findley, photo courtesy the author. **Back endpaper**—Map of Pearl Harbor, Library of Congress.

HISTORICAL SOURCES: World War II produced a trove of historical volumes and materials. Especially useful in preparing this book were: *The Glory and the Dream,* by William Manchester; Time-Life's *This Fabulous Century* series, for the decades of the 1920s, '30s, and '40s; *The Age of Roosevelt,* vols. II and III, by Arthur M. Schlesinger, Jr.; *History of United States Naval Operations in World War II,* vol. I, by Samuel Eliot Morrison; *Chronicle of the 20th Century,* Clifton Daniel, Editor-in-Chief; Gordon W. Prange's *At Dawn We Slept—the Untold Story of Pearl Harbor,* and *Pearl Harbor, the Verdict of History*; John Toland's *Adolf Hitler,* vols. I and II; *The Battle of the Atlantic* volume from Time-Life's World War II series; and "Yesterday, December 7, 1941. . .", by Richard Ketchum, in *American Heritage,* November, 1989. Many other fascinating books and articles are available in your public library.